Breaking Free:
A Handbook for Recovery from Family Abuse and Violence

Esly Regina Carvalho, Ph.D.

**TraumaClinic
Edições**

Breaking Free:
A handbook for Recovery from Family Abuse and Violence

Esly Regina Carvalho, Ph.D.

TraumaClinic Edições

Breaking Free: *A handbook for recovery from family abuse and violence*

ISBN-13: 978-1941727164
ISBN-10: 1941727166

Cover: Claudio Ferreira
Layout: Esly Regina Carvalho, Ph.D.
Translation into English: Judith Jones

TraumaClinic Edições
SEPS 705/905 Ed. Santa Cruz sala 441
70.390-755 Brasília, DF Brasil
WWW.traumaclinicedicoes.com.br

Acknowledgements

We would like to thank the team of the Ecuadorian Center for the Promotion and Action for *Women (Centro Ecuatoriano para la Promoción y Ación de la Mujer — CEPAM)* for their contribution, as well as the participants of the groups that met in the safe house during 1991-92, when this material was being used in their women's shelter for those coming out of situations of violence. Special thanks to Ana Maria Oviedo, Myriam Graces and Anna Cristina Ruiz.

Dedicated to...

...all of the women who have had the courage to break the silence of their situation...

...and to those who would like to do it....

Index

Index 7

Introduction 9

Initial Considerations 11

Introduction 13

A. My relationships 17
   1. My Family of Origin 17
   2. My Present-Day Family 19
   3. My Personal Life 21

B. My relationships with myself 23
   4. My Body 23
   5. My Sexuality 25
   6. My Feelings 27
   7. My Spirituality 29

C. My husband (partner) and I 31
   8. What we are going through right now 31
   9. Female/Male 33
   10. History of our Marriage 35
   11. The Sexual Relationship of the Couple 37
   12. Violence 39

D. Freedom 41
   13. My Future 41
   14. My Sons and Daughters 43
   15. A Letter 45
   16. Violence 47
   17. Breaking Free 49

Conclusion 51

Guide for Facilitators: How to Use This Material 53

Some rules about group meetings: For Facilitators 59

Why do Women Tolerate Violence? 63

Recommendations for Facilitators 67

Professional Help for 69

Additional Resources and Tools 73

About the Author 75

Introduction

In 1992, a women's shelter opened as a result of the work of the Ecuadorian Center for the Promotion and Action of Women *Women (Centro Ecuatoriano para la Promoción y Ación de la Mujer – CEPAM)* in Quito, Ecuador. It was for women and children, victims of domestic violence and sexual abuse. This shelter became an institutional landmark in the country. In conjunction with the Pastoral Office for Family, Women and Children of the Latin American Council of Churches – CLAI), it produced a methodology that was first of its kind with regard to the problem of violence in the family. It incorporated the technical knowledge and practical studies that had already been previously established, and blended it with the experiential and transformational method of Psychodrama in a Christian context.

Ecuadorian psychologist and psychotherapist, **Ana Matilde Oviedo**, finished her studies in Spain and Sweden where she worked for long periods with victims of organized violence. She was part of the team of CEPAM that that headed the work in the women's shelter.

Brazilian psychodramatist and clinical psychologist, **Esly Regina Carvalho**, Ph.D., a specialist in the theory and practice of sociodrama, psychodrama and sociometry, developed the methodology. She had already written books and manuals about difficulties that affect the family in today's world, such as divorce, the issues that children of separated/divorced parents face; people living with HIV/AIDS and other issues along these lines..

Social worker and psychodramatist **Anna Cristina Ruiz**, was part of the team that worked directly with the women in the pilot project that validated this methodology.

Now translated into English, this manual is offered to communities and institutions that work alongside the women who grapple with this problem. We want to help with the treatment and recovery of people who are victims of the violence which ultimately affects all of us. It is our desire that we can contribute to the effort of putting an end to the cycle of violence in our country.

If you would like to keep abreast of what we are developing in this area, feel free to write us so that you can receive our newsletters. We send occasional notes with recommendations and suggestions, news and resources.

Here is the link: **http://tinyurl.com/mhtd2hz**

Initial Considerations

"I opened the door for my lover, but he had already gone. How I wanted to hear his voice! I looked for him, but couldn't find him; I called to him, but heard no answer. The sentries patrolling the city found me; they struck me and bruised me; the guards at the city wall tore off my cape."

Song of Solomon 5:6-7 (Good News Translation).

This passage shows us that even the Bible mentions the violence perpetrated against women. In this short quotation from the Song of Solomon we see several presuppositions and myths that, unfortunately, even today contribute to the issue of abuse against women:

1. A woman, found at night on the street, cannot possibly be considered a virtuous woman; therefore, the men who find her can do what they want with her.

2. A woman is an "object" without value, and therefore, she can be used by men; they can be taken advantage of her sexually, take off her clothes, and to hit her "serves her right" as popular thinking often goes.

3. Even though a woman maintains her innocence, she is "always" guilty: she was where she should not have been, with whom she should not have been, at an hour when she should not be out and about, doing what she should not be doing. If she were "a good girl" or "an honorable woman," none of this would have happened to her.

From the times of Solomon and the Shulammite to the present day, very little seems to have changed regarding the women's roles. There is still a double standard: no matter what she says, she will always be the guilty one in any situation.

It is very sad to have to say that, even today, women continue to be the victims of social, economic and domestic violence. They continue to be sequestered in their homes by silence: wrongly thinking that, if they keep quiet about it, one day their husband will change miraculously and they will be able to finally live in peace.

We believe it is our job to break the silence. We believe that we must raise a prophetic voice and denounce the terrible secret of family violence. We ought to accompany those involved in this situation so that they can find healthy solutions and resolve their conflicts by finding new forms of family communication.

It is towards this end that we offer this simple notebook. We hope that the people who make use of it can contribute towards therapeutic interventions in the lives of those who are victims of family violence.

Introduction

In this notebook, we deal with one of the best-kept secrets: violence within the family. Because family relationships have hues and tones regarding power and affection, as well as inter-dependency among all of their members, there is fertile ground whereby violence can grow. Perhaps psychological and verbal abuse are the most common forms of violence. And we know that in general, it is the women, both as adults and as children, who suffer the most from these situations.

Violence is defined by Geles and Strauss as "an intervention or an act used in order to do harm or humiliate another person. Violence is the intention of a person to use physical and/or verbal force to show their desire to put an end to a conflict. Violence exists within a relationship of domination of one person over another, using subtle and/or clear means to cause apathy and make the other person back down." (*Society and Change in Family Violence,* 1975-85).

The phenomenon of marital violence demonstrates the oppression of women within our present-day societies by means of social and economic laws, many of which still have a patriarchal bent (especially in Latin America). There are social, economical and ideological conditioning that marks the tensions and confrontations in the interaction between family members. This often leads to the power struggles that often mark relationships between the sexes, and unfortunately, contribute towards the legitimizing the victimization of women. It prepares them from infancy, for a life of passivity and dedication to others; the underlying lesson is one of humbling or sacrificing themselves for the good of others, often with feelings of guilt and a sense of not having any options whereby they can express themselves or choose according to their own needs.

On the other hand, violent men perceive their loss of control as something that legitimizes their attitude. All it takes is for his wife to refuse to fulfill one of his desires for him to justify the use of physical or psychological humiliations.

Maybe the physical humiliation is the more visible and less "hurtful," but it goes along with a dose of psychological violence that carries the risk of disastrous endings. Psychological violence is the less visible, but more insidious form of abuse, since it lowers self-esteem. It reduces the personal value of the person in their own eyes. This is one of the reasons that an abused woman needs an enormous amount of support in order to believe in her own abilities. It takes a while for her to begin to believe in herself, allow her self-esteem to grow, be respected, and realize that she also has rights as a human being. A violent man also needs to learn new and healthy forms of relationship and communication.

Hope is reborn in the heart of every abused woman when she is able to grow in the belief that she can find a viable solution to end the violence in her life. For men who wish to change, hope arises when they are able to recognize that the destructive patterns in which he is involved keep him from fulfilling his true potential, for both himself and for his family. Reaching these goals is not an easy task.

We hope that working through the exercises in this notebook will help people reach their goals of living a better life, in peace and harmony.

A. My relationships

1. My Family of Origin

So that we can understand where we are going, it is necessary to know from where we came. Below, draw a picture of your original family: the people who took care of you, your mother, your father, brothers and sisters or the people who took over these roles in your life. Don't worry if it is not a beautiful picture. The majority does not know how to draw better than a six-year-old. The important thing is that you can express what you want to say.

Now, think a bit about your drawing. How may people are included? What expressions do they have? What are the feelings that your drawing transmits? If you are participating in a group, share with the others a bit about the significance of living in this family.

Additional questions:
- How many people form part of your family? Describe them: your father, your mother, your brothers and sisters, your husband, other people who are significant in your life, like a grandmother, or a maid.

- What do you think of your family? What adjective would you use to describe the climate at home? What did you like best in your family? What did you like least? How did you spend your free time in your family?

2. My Present-Day Family

Make a drawing of the family you are in today.

Who makes up your family? How are they organized in your drawing? Did you forget to include someone? What feelings does your drawing bring up? If you could describe your family with one adjective, what would it be? Are there any changes you would like to make in your drawing? Which ones?

Additional questions:
- What does your husband/partner do? How would you describe him/her? What do you do in your free time? Do you have a job? What do you do?

- Describe each of your children.

- How is your relationship with other family members? How is your relationship with your extended family?

3. My Personal Life

Make a drawing of the things that are important to you:
include people, things, attributes, etc., everything counts.
Distribute everything on your sheet as you feel they are
organized in your life.

Does your drawing have a lot of things? Or just a few? Is your life full of things that you like? Or only the things that you need to do in order to survive? Are there many colors? Looking at your drawing: what conclusion can you draw from it? What are the changes that you would like to make? Which ones are possible?

Additional questions:
- What adjective can you use to describe your present life? What does that mean to you?

- What do you imagine that people think about you? Do they take you into consideration when they make a decision? Whose opinions influence you the most?

How many friends do you have? Do you confide in others?

4. My Body

Make a drawing of your body. It doesn't matter if it comes out crooked...few people are artists. Use colored pencils, if possible, and try to reflect on what you feel about your body.

So… what do you think? What are the parts that you like the most? that you like the least? What seems to be most beautiful? And what do you find ugly? What are the special characteristics that make your body yours? With what word would you describe it? Do you like this drawing?

Additional questions::
- Does your body work well? How do you feel during your periods? Did your body change after you had children?

- What do you think that your husband/partner thinks about your body? What about other people?

- How does your perception of your body affect your sexuality?

Additional exercise:
Ask the people to look at their whole body in a mirror. Ask each one how they feel, what they see, what there is that is positive. Allow the others in the group to also say something *positive. (No negative language allowed!)*

5. My Sexuality

Imagine that your sexuality is an animal. What animal would it be? Do you like this animal? Why or why not? What does this animal mean to you?

Now draw this animal and write a short story about it. What does this animal have to do with your sexuality? In what way can you explain what you feel?

Additional questions:

- What did they teach you about sex when you were a child? How did they teach you? How did you find out about sex? Are there other experiences in this area that you would like to share?

- Many children were sexually abused when they were children. Did this happen to you? Do not be ashamed to talk about this. Children are not to blame for what was done to them when they were little. But the secret and the effort to hide this information is what can cause us problems.

6. My Feelings

If you are participating in a group, try to share a bit about the feelings connected to your experiences. In general, it is very hard to talk about that which hurts us.. At times, we are ashamed to speak of that which we already went through, or worse, what we have had to put up with.

We believe that it is important to talk about these things, at least about the things that we have already felt and gone through. To not talk about them many times means that the emotional poison from these feelings continues to kill us, little by little. Talking is a way to let go and to heal. Therefore, try to talk about it, as much (or as little) as you can. Talk about what you are able to, even though it is just a bit.

(If you like, you can copy the questions on a separate piece of paper to distribute to the group.)

One of the feelings that exists within me is........................

The feeling that I have that I like the most is........................

When I am angry I feel...

I want to cry when...

Additional questions:
- What is the predominant feeling that you are experiencing this very moment?

- What do you think about feelings? Are they friends or enemies? How could they help you in this moment?

7. My Spirituality

Our spirituality is an important part of our lives. This is how we connect with God (however we perceive Him). We know that it is not possible to represent the full extent of a relationship with God on a piece of paper, but it is helpful to have an idea of what our emotional relationship with God is like. Putting it on paper can be an eye-opening exercise.

Make a drawing of your relationship with God and other significant spiritual elements in your life at this moment. Don't think too much. Just do it!

Is God present in your life? Do you believe that He can help in some way? How? Is there someone who could give you some spiritual help? Who? How?

Additional questions:
- What does spirituality mean in your life? What were you taught about God when you were a child? about the Church? Do you believe that someone could help you in this situation? Who? How?

C. My husband (partner) and I

8. What we are going through right now

Make a drawing of you and your husband (partner) and what it's like right now.

How are you today? What word describes you? Are you near each other or a long way off? What expression do you have? Do you wish that your relationship were different? In what ways?

Additional question:
- How did you meet? What was your relationship like soon after you were married? What has changed? How did things begin to change? What are you like today?

9. Female/Male

Make two drawings, one of a man, the other of a woman. In your drawing, try to express the differences that are between the two.

What are the differences that you perceive in your drawings? Comparing your drawing with those of your colleagues in your group, what do you perceive? what do they have in common? what differences?

Additional questions:
- Do you believe that men have certain rights that women do not have? What would they be? Do women have rights that men do not have? What would they be?

- Should sons be brought up differently from daughters? Why? In what ways?

- If you have brothers and sisters, did your parents treat them differently? How?

10. History of our Marriage

How did you meet? How did you decide to marry/live together? Make a time line and point out the important moments.

Share with your group about your courtship and marriage. How did you arrive at where you are now?

11. The Sexual Relationship of the Couple

Make a drawing of two animals that represent you and your husband (partner), and your sexual relationship.

Suggestions:

It could be difficult to talk about sexual relationship, but it is very important to do so. Be sure that everyone has all of the correct information they need in order to make good decisions regarding sex. If you can, invite a doctor, nurse or psychologist to come and give a lesson, and answer questions.

12. Violence

Make a drawing of what violence means to you.

What feelings come up for you when you look at this? What do you remember? What experiences have you had where violence was present? When did this happen? At what age? How did you feel?
Additional questions:

- Why do you think that you are abused? In what kinds of situations does the abuse occur? How do you react? Are there witnesses to it? Do you do something? Is it possible to do something? Do you think you deserve it?

If there are men present in the meeting:
What do you think is the reason why you resort to violence? How do you react? What is it that bothers you? How do you feel afterwards?

Additional exercises:
- Women: Make a drawing of yourself after having been abused.

- Men: Make a drawing of you after you have abused someone.

D. Freedom

13. My Future

Make a drawing of how you imagine the future will be with your mate. Do not put down the ideal situation, or how you would like for it to be, but draw what you really believe will be your future with him if nothing changes.

What do you perceive? Do you like what you see? Comment with your group.

If you do not see your future with good eyes, stop and think a bit about why it seems that it will be so difficult to introduce changes. What does it depend on? What can you change in the present to change the future?

14. My Sons and Daughters

Make a drawing of your sons and daughters.

What do you perceive about your sons and daughters? How are they distributed in the drawing? Who is near whom? Who is well liked? Who is not well liked? Describe each of your sons and daughters with one adjective. If possible, share this with the others in group.

Comment:
It is very important that people can put themselves in the place of their sons and daughters, so that they can feel and perceive what their children feel and perceive. Many for the sake of our children that we are not willing or able to make for ourselves. Our sons and daughters can become a strong reason to motivate us towards change. This is not supposed to give us a guilt trip, OK?

15. A Letter

Imagine that you are one of your sons or one of your daughters. Write your name here: _____.

Now write a letter to "your mother" telling her how you feel, living in this family: how you see her, how you see your father, the situations that you are going through, etc., but from the perspective of your son or your daughter. If you prefer doing the exercise as a dramatization, it can be done that way as well. Have the "son" or "daughter" sit in a different chair, and "interview" them about what they fell like, living in this family.

What do you perceive about your family situation from the perspective of your son or daughter? Share.

Are there changes that you would like to make? Which ones? How?

16. Violence

Now comes a time when we can evaluate the choices and alternatives that are available to us when handling the situation of violence and abuse.

How can I face this situation in a better way? What are my choices?

a. Internal resources

What things can I change in me that would have repercussions in the relationship with someone who abuses me? In other words, what are the things that I do that facilitate or stir up the situations of violence? Is this realistic?

b. External resources

What are some external resources that are within my reach?
- in my community, church, neighborhood, friends?
- in my own family?

It is very important to reflect on these possibilities because one can control how one is going to confront the situation of violence in one's life. A woman can close herself off to others and lose even more self-esteem, or take the initiative to do something for herself and her family. Remember that the victims of violence are not the only ones who suffer: one should also try to get help for the violent person.

It is imperative to try to identify the factors that contribute to maintaining the situation of violence so that one can begin to disarm them. It is encouraging to learn that there are more internal and external resources available that one doesn't always remember when the panic sets in. Learning to exercise these resources is one of the important steps in getting out of the abusive situation.

.

17. Breaking Free

Now you will have an opportunity to make an evaluation of your life. You have already had the chance to think about many different subjects in these past few weeks. You can share your experiences from working this journal. Perhaps new things will come up as well.

How do you want your life to be from here on out?

What expectations do you have?

How can you make these things happen?

Do you need help? From whom? In what way?

It is important to learn to evaluate. Once you have learned this, you can stop and evaluate your life whenever necessary, even when you no longer meet in the group. It is a tool that will become a part of your life. Pinpointing what our situation is like, and what factors go into it will help us discover the choices for change. We need to be aware of what is going on in our lives in order to bring in the change.

Conclusion

We hope that this notebook has been useful to you. We believe that this should not be just a bunch of exercise, but a lifestyle change, where you learn to reflect and analyze the things that are happening to you. It is important to know that many times we exercise more control over many aspects of our lives than we initially thought. When we do not change some things in our lives, we become part of the problem by maintaining situations that can be bad for us (and for children).

We want to encourage you to continue your process of emotional growth. It is fundamental that you have a clear vision of what you want out of life, and move towards reaching those goals.

We hope that this notebook will continue to guide you in your search to find a life full of dignity and new opportunities.

Guide for Facilitators:

How to Use This Material

This material was developed for those who are affected by domestic violence. It is a working notebook, as you can see, and not simply a book to be read. The idea is that people can reflect on the questions presented here and bring clarity into the situations in their lives.

Ideally, this book should be worked in small groups with a maximum of 12 people. Meetings can be held up to 3 times a week(in situations where the people want or need others to walk with them in a more intense manner, like when they are in a shelter or receiving court-ordered psychological counseling),. More often, meetings will be once a week, when people are working on their problems while still living at home.

We suggest that the meetings have a set time to start and finish. Two hours is an ideal time-frame. Meetings should be held in a place where there are no interruptions and there is no risk of being overheard. Children should not be present so that the adults can talk freely about whatever they want to.

We were careful to make the notebook in such a way that those who do not know how to read and write can also use it with great benefit. With some modifications, you can use the material to work with men, if that should be necessary. (One of our experiences in Quito was that several men asked for help in order to save their marriage.) When illiterate people participate, the facilitator should read the instructions so that everyone can follow along. When the notebook describes an exercise that requires writing, a drawing can be substituted, or a role-laying of the situation. People who do like to write and draw can take advantage of their notebooks and make them a kind of journal where they write down their comments. Warn participants that they need to put away their notebooks in a private place where no one else will find it. It is not something for others to read.

It is advisable to do the first lesson together so participants can understand the methodology. To save time, people can fill in their notebooks as and bring them to group meetings for sharing.

No one should be pressured to speak or share if they are not comfortable or ready. These meetings are to discuss issues that are difficult and painful. Each person should be allowed to work at their own speed, their own way. On the other hand, sharing about what is going can be healing and therapeutic. One of the complicated aspects surrounding violence and abuse is the secrecy. If we learn to talk about it, we break the power of secrecy. This is very healing in itself. Encourage all to participate, but do not pressure anyone.

Some rules about group meetings:

1. Maintain confidentiality. This is essential. When you begin meetings where people will be sharing their personal details, keeping the content private is fundamental to the success of proposal. If someone new comes into the group, it is important to emphasize that everything that happens in the group is confidential.

Let participants share at their own pace. When dealing with feelings linked to issues of violence plus family loyalty, not everyone will feel comfortable sharing right off the bat. Knowing that no one will share their stories outside the group is important in order to encourage their confidence and trust in the group. This will enable them to talk about things that they never told anyone.

Another reason why confidentiality is so important is protection and safety for group members. If word gets back to the abuser it can mean further violence. For example, if a husband hears that details of his behavior had been commented in a group discussion, it could lead to heated arguments and possibly bring on more violence. This is something we want to avoid at all costs.

2. Commit to participating. Don't miss meetings except under emergency situations. In order to grow together it is necessary to be together. Healing comes from feeling the solidarity of others. Nothing kills a group off faster than intermittent participation.

3. Do not give suggestions or advice. Each person is doing the best they can. We don't live better because we do not know how to live better. That is the whole point of the group meetings. There would be no reason to get together around this topic if we already had all of the answers! People are often stuck, trapped, in situations that do not have an easy solution. If they knew how to resolve the situation, they would have done it already. Be careful not to tell people what to do, nor let others do so with each other.

4. Confess only your own faults. We can spend *centuries* complaining about others. People involved in abusive relationships are not guilty of the abuse. And we know that the abuser also needs help. It is a complete waste of time if the group members only complain about what is going on. We cannot change other people. We can only change ourselves.

On the other hand, a person should be able to share their feelings and facts that are relevant to what they are going through. To narrate a situation is different from complaining about others.

5. Accept what is said, especially when a person shares their feelings. If you are not able to open up with one another in this group, where will you do it? Each person has the right to feel what they feel. No arguments. No recrimination or "oh, but you shouldn't feel like that".

6. Have a set time to begin and end. Stick to the schedule. Participants can get in trouble at home if they are late. The stress around scheduling issues can be so great that it could be the deciding factor in a participant's decision not to return.

7. If someone shows strong emotions (crying, anger, fury, etc.) let them express it. Do not be afraid of strong emotions. It is possible that others in the group also have difficulty dealing with their own responses when facing these feelings. Oftentimes strong emotions have become associated with abuse, and fury with violence. It is necessary to learn differentiate between them. A person can be angry without this being expressed in violence, and can cry without this leading to depression.

8. Allow participants to speak, but do not make anyone share. Be careful not to let the same speak all the time, but be careful to divide the time in such a way that all who want to speak can do so.

Finally, for some of those who are working in a group setting, they should have the option of leaving their notebooks in the meeting place, of possible, to avoid having others find and read it. For those who work alone, we suggest that you write or draw in your notebook, and find a safe place for it. Perhaps you can find another person with whom you could share what you wrote, someone in whom you can confide. It needs to be someone who will listen to you, and help you think through what is going on.

For Facilitators

Before one starts to work with women in situations of abuse, it is important to know understand some of the myths, stereotypes, and family dynamics concerning this issue..

There is a lot to learn about the family dynamics involved with abuse and violence. We encourage those who want to do this kind of work to read up on the literature this issue. We know that relationships of power, control and emotional dependence are established amongst members of any family, but in families of abuse, the common factor tends to be that women, both as adults and as children, are victims of abuse by men.

The violence of which we speak is not just physical; many women complain more about psychological abuse than about their bruises.

Many thanks come together that eventually lead to domestic violence. One of the aspects that concerns us most is the fact that children who are abuse or see abuse in childhood often repeat the model with which they have become familiar. Men learn to abuse and see this as their right and privilege; women learn to tolerate and put up with it. Sometimes they think in some strange way that they are guilty and responsible for the abuse, and often think that they are deserving of it.

So we take this opportunity to mention some of the popular myths regarding domestic violence. First in line is the idea that women are attacked, abused or assaulted because she did something to provoke the man. She is therefore "guilty" and directly responsible for the violence and abuse. This is a myth that even the some professionals repeat, putting an even greater load of guilt on the woman than that which she already carries. We see that among abused women in general they believe that they "deserve" such treatment. Their self-esteem is so low that they have begun to believe that they do not deserve to be treated with respect and dignity; therefore, their tolerance for violence has reached an incredible level.

The second myth is that women like to be beaten, as if they were some kind of "masochists" by nature. In extreme cases, we have heard that to hit a woman is a sign of love(!): "A husband who loves his wife should beat her up." There are some cultures that have a greater tolerance towards domestic violence, but one cannot continue to maintain the myth that women like this type of treatment. It never does anyone any good and we are well aware of cases where women have died at the hands of their uncontrolled husbands/partners. We are also familiar with situations where women went to jail because she eventually killed her partner in self-defense, after years of violence and abuse. Yet in Latin America many husbands get off scot-free when they kill their wives because they "have the "right to "wash their honor with blood".

For this reason we talk about "double load of suffering" that abuse women often carry: the violence itself, and the silence of the family and of society (and of some religious institutions...) regarding what is happening in the intimacy of the home. The social tolerance and protection offered to the abuser perpetuates it for lack of an outcry and appropriate intervention. All of these myths and preconceived ideas contribute to the isolation of abused women, who often resign themselves to their situations as victims of never-ending violence.

Third, there is no such thing as a "typical psychological profile" of abused women. They do not stand out from the general population (except for the occasional bruises, black eyes they try to cover with make-up or broken limbs from "a fall). Women in situations of abuse can be found in all socio-economic levels of society, whatever their level of schooling. Unfortunately, we know that there are abused women even in the church, hiding their terrible secrets.

Why do Women

Tolerate Violence?

As mentioned earlier, for some women abuse was the family model with which they grew up. For some women, to live in a family meant living with violence. They did not perceive that there were other ways to live even though they would have liked to know about them.

Sometimes, putting up with violence and abuse was a way of maintaining the nuclear family. There are socio-cultural factors that contribute towards the maintenance of this belief yet today. Popular sayings or proverbs contribute exemplify it. In Ecuador, there are those who say "He is the husband is: even if he hits me, even if he kills me, he is the husband." (*Marido es: aunque pegue, aunque mate, marido es).* Mothers, aunts, and even other women in the family will often insist that women should to put up with the abuse (and do so quietly) so as to maintain the "family unity". In Brazil, there is a refrain that goes, "It's bad with him; it's worse without him" (*Mal com ele, pior sem ele*). As a result, women are taught that they are incapable of living without a man's presence in their lives, no matter how bad he is. It is more important to have a man in one's life who is bad, than to not have one at all. In Peru it is said that the more one hits a wife, the more he shows his love (*"más me pega, más me ama".)*

Female stereotypes promoted by both family and society insist that women ought to be sweet, passive, and serve their families, etc. This makes women even more vulnerable to violence, developing passive attitudes in the face of violence and abuse.

Some religious beliefs contribute to the maintenance of family violence. There are still some Christian denominations that do not permit divorce or separation under any circumstances. Women who would like to leave their husbands because of violence will have to confront social and ecclesiastical rejection precisely at a time when they are especially vulnerable and fragile. We earnestly believe that every pastor or priest should think twice and respond in the fear of God before counseling a woman to return to her home and husband who abuses her (and the children) physically. All of us are well aware of instances where this resulted in the women's death.

Recent studies also have demonstrated how trauma "freezes" memory in the brain. (Remember Lot's wife?) To a certain degree, trauma makes people repeat behavior. Violence begets trauma and trauma begets violence. The good news is that now there are scientific treatment that can heal traumas and free people from patterns of violence. Today, EMDR therapy (Eye Movement Desensitization and Reprocessing)[1] offers relief. These terrible memories from the past can be transformed, healing them at the level of neurochemistry.

For these and other reasons, this notebook is part of an effort to help women nurture new meaning for their lives. We hope they grow in their self-esteem; that they can learn to value to themselves as a person, as a woman, as a mother, as a professional. Hopefully, these exercises

---

[1] See www.emdr.com

will help women gain a new perspective about themselves, their families and to their situations.

Our desire is that these women may find alternative solutions that are healthier. We want to help them break the "sound barrier" (silence and secrecy) that has held so many in quiet torture.

Finally, we hope that as women are able to change their situations, they will be able to transmit to the abuser the fact that he, too, needs help. It is necessary that men perceive that this form of family communication is harmful to them as well. They deprive themselves of the option of resolving their conflicts in a healthy manner. And, in the final analysis, they deprive themselves of a happy family life that so many desire.

Recommendations for Facilitators

We believe that it is not necessary to be a health professional in order to develop the role of facilitator with groups working on the issue of abuse and domestic violence. In fact, we believe that the best facilitators are exactly those people who have passed through these experiences and have walked away to freedom and emotional health. We believe in the work of the lay person, but we also understand that it is important to have continual training regarding the issue at hand.

A facilitators needs to have some characteristics and abilities that we consider very essential:

1. Be impartial. Do not make moral judgments. A person who has not gone through what the other person is experiencing will find it difficult to believe or feel what that person is feeling. It is not right to add guilt to suffering. Some people will leave a group for this reasons and rightly so.

2. Be sensitive, empathic and compassionate. Do not ask questions out of curiosity. Questions ought to be asked only to clear up what is happening or what the other person is feeling. Ask the individual how you can help.

3. Listen. When you have stopped listening, listen some more. You do not have to have the answers or feel that you have to give solutions. We cannot give ourselves the role of God, the All Powerful. The temptation to end the suffering of a person could make us want to find a solution for everything. One must not succumb to this temptation. Besides, if we do everything for the other person, we deprive them of the possibility of learning to solve their own problems. Intervention should be limited to situations of life and death, and/or physical danger for the persons involved.

4. Use simple language. It is very important to speak clearly and use simple language. You should not be embarrassed to speak, clear up and clarify significant aspects of what is being shared, as necessary.

5. Be informed about places for immediate help in **your community**, like shelters for women with and without children. Also pull together a list of people that help people in urgent situations: doctors, nurses or others in the health community. Know where, when and how to send them there safely. Visit these places and talk with the people in charge so you know them personally. Fin out how these places work and how you ought to guide those in need. It also helps for you to be able to explain to the person what awaits them when they get there in case you are not able to go with them.

6. Know about the laws that govern issues of violence. Make a note of the important facts in case one day you are called upon to testify, always maintaining confidentiality.

Finally, it is important to note that the work with this kind of population brings its risks. What happens is fairly unforeseeable at times. It is important to take this into account so that you do not create unnecessary anguish - in the facilitator or amongst the participants.

Professional Help for
People Coming Out of Violence and Abuse

One of the things that is slowly changing the face of professional treatment for those coming out of violence are the new reprocessing psychotherapies, especially EMDR therapy. Scientifically proven to treat Post-Traumatic Stress Disorder (PTSD) , it is a relatively fast and efficient form of treating and resolving traumatic experiences. Since we know that those coming out of violence and abuse have gone through situations of great risk and vulnerability, EMDR has become the therapy of choice to treat people at risk for PTSD.

EMDR therapy (Eye Movement Desensitization and Reprocessing) was discovered and developed by Dr. Francine Shapiro in 1987, in the United States. Since then, more than one hundred thousand therapists worldwide have been trained in an approach that represents a change of paradigm in psychotherapy. In Brazil alone there are more than 1,500 trained therapists.

If we understand that traumas, nightmares and bad memories of adverse situations are stored in a mal-adaptive form in the brain networks, then we can begin to understand how EMDR can reprocess these fears, phobias, terrors, and anxieties that are connected to painful memories that keep victims trapped by these ghosts from the past. This is accomplished by the integration of reprocessed information that was once in separate parts of the brain. In an accelerated and adaptive manner, EMDR seems to "imitate" what happens to people as they go through the REM (Rapid

Eye Movement) phases of the sleep cycle. This is the phase when the brain processes daily life and stores it in an adaptive form, then transforms it into past memory. For reasons that are not totally understood, in some situations people are not able to process this information in a normal and healthy manner. Perhaps this is the origin of nightmares, startle responses, intrusive and obsessive thoughts, or post-traumatic stress disorder (PTSD) and its consequences. In some cases, people can develop Dissociative Identity Disorder (DID) as a result of chronic, repetitive and constant traumas (such as incest) that occur during childhood.

In order to apply EMDR, the psychotherapist needs to have been duly trained in accredited courses, where both EMDR theory as well as the practice of the eight phases of EMDR therapy are taught along with three-pronged (past, present and future) protocol. Trained therapists learn how to evaluate the indication (or lack thereof) for EMDR therapy; how to develop a treatment plan; and how to conceptualize the diagnosis and treatment according to Adaptive Information Processing which is the theoretical basis for EMDR.

At the present time, there are more than 200 scientific studies with rigorous clinical methodology and an indexed journal specifically dedicated to the study of EMDR (*Journal of EMDR Practice and Research*[2]) that scientifically. The World Health Organization (WHO) has approved EMDR therapy as one of two efficacious psychotherapies in the treatment of post-traumatic stress. It has the seal of the *National Registry of*

---

[2] http: www.springerpub.com/product/19333196

Evidence-based Programs and Practices (NREPP) of the North American government.[2] The scientific proof for EMDR therapy is undeniable.[3-4]

Because this chapter refers to professional treatment, we will not enter into greater detail in this manual, since the goal here is to offer a tool that even lay people can use. But the work would be incomplete if we did not inform readers that there already are efficient methods of treating traumas and the difficult consequences of it.

---

[3] http: nrepp.samhsa.gov/ViewIntervention.aspx?id=199
[4] SEe a complete list of research on www.emdr.com

Additional Resources and Tools

If you would like to receive more information through correspondence, sign on to our list:
http://tinyurl.com/mhtd2hz

Other books by Esly Regina Carvalho, Ph.D.

Healing the Folks Who Live Inside.
http://tinyurl.com/ntucl7s
Do you sometimes feel like you don't understand your reactions, feelings or thoughts? As if someone had hijacked the driver's seat of your life and you wound up doing something stupid? Or regret your response? You don't make sense in some situations, even to yourself? *Maybe a wounded inner role took over and you didn't catch it...?* This book will explain what you can do about it.

Bibliodrama Manual . **http://tinyurl.com/ntos97u**
This manual was written to help those people who are interested in developing Bibliodrama in their churches, synagogues and communities. It makes Bible stories come alive! Enriched by Peter Pitzele's midrashic form of Bibliodrama, this manual will tell you what Bibliodrama is, its form, techniques and structures, as well as suggestions for how to conduct them. Full of practical ideas and suggestions, it will guide you from simple to more advanced forms of conducting Bibliodramas. Included is how to do Playback of

Biblical stories, an art form specifically developed by this author.

When the Bond Breaks. http://tinyurl.com/puq328o
In her personal inimitable style, the author invites the readers to adopt an attitude that is consistent with the grace of God, who hates the sin of divorce, but loves the divorced. Esly shares from her own experience of divorce and remarriage, the challenges, difficulties and issues that need to be overcome in order to become a more whole human being.

Check out Esly's books in Spanish and Portuguese as well on her Amazon Author page:
amazon.com/author/eslycarvalho

**Leave your review of this book on
Amazon so that other people can take advantage of
your opinion. It is greatly appreciated!**

http://tinyurl.com/nqgafws

About the Author

For more than 20 years, **Esly Regina de Carvalho, Ph.D.,** has dedicated herself to the area of emotional healing: as a psychologist in private practice; as a teacher, offering training in several therapeutic modalities, such as EMDR therapy, Brainspotting, and Psychodrama; as an author, sharing and communicating her experience with others; and as a public speaker in great demand. She is committed to helping people overcome the challenges of life,. She has worked in Brazil, as well as in other countries of Latin America, the United States, Portugal, and Spain.

Esly Carvalho maintained a private practice in the Dallas area for many years before her return to Brazil in 2006. A Brazilian-American clinical psychologist and author, her practice grew into the TraumaClinic, located in Brasilia, which treats clients who suffer from trauma, depression and anxiety. She also spends extended time training EMDR professionals in several countries.

An international trainer and speaker in great demand, Esly has also published books and articles about the use of EMDR and Psychodrama (her first training approach). She was responsible for founding the Psychodrama movement in Ecuador in 1990, which now boasts several training groups and hosted the 7th Ibero-American Psychodrama conference in 2009, in Quito, Ecuador. She also took the EMDR movement to that country, and the EMDR Ecuador national organization hosted the II Iberian-American EMDR Conference in 2010

Esly is a published author in three languages, and several of her books have become international bestsellers. Her latest book, **_Healing the Folks Who Live Inside,_** will soon receive a sequel, with more case studies pertaining to healing from trauma associated with disease, diagnosis, and medical interventions.

Esly is dedicated to developing a generation of professionals who are committed to emotional health and healing, and to alleviating the pain of those who suffer.

After living many years in the United States, Ecuador and Bolivia, Esly is presently settled in Brasília, Brazil, where she directs the **TraumaClinic** do Brasil, (www.traumaclinic.com.br) specialized in treating trauma, anxiety, and depression with EMDR therapy. Esly is married and enjoys being a grandmother.

www.ingramcontent.com/pod-product-compliance
Lightning Source LLC
Chambersburg PA
CBHW020602030426
42337CB00013B/1171